Live a Purposeful Life with Passion

"When you change the way you look at things, the things you look at change!"...Dr. Wayne Dyer

<u>Affirmation</u>

"I allow the power of intention to unfold through me."

Dedicated To Your Higher Self

Peace and Blessings

A wise friend once sent me a quote by Winston Churchill: **"Success is going from failure to failure without loss of enthusiasm."** After reading this quote, my mind went into hundreds of different directions. After silencing my mind, I started to reflect on its numerous implications. I thought to myself how relevant and powerful this message was to what I was experiencing. Having struggled in my career to become licensed as a physician and simultaneously recovering from an unsuccessful relationship, I was not in tune with my inner self, how I dealt with my emotions and what my priorities were in life. I reached a point in my life where I felt I had no choice but to make a shift from the outward to the inward. I started meditating to 'Japa', a spiritual discipline involving the meditative repetition of a mantra or name of God, 'AHH'. My life gradually started changing for the better. Being inspired, I began reading quotes and mantras written by enlightened spiritual beings, who expressed themselves with tremendous beauty and truth and manifested their divinity through love and powerful language. I read numerous books to educate myself in the field of personal development in order to acquire as many tools and techniques in my life as possible. Over time, it became a habit for me to wake up very early in the morning, create a special and serene time to meditate, read soul inspiring quotes from authors whom I felt

My Reflection

----

guided me from a place deep inside my being and then share my thoughts and feelings on my social media, Facebook. Gradually, this practice gave me the inspirational boost of spiritual, physical and emotional energy to enhance my day and motivated me to do better, think better, feel better and transmit that joyous feeling to my friends.

As time went by, I began to create my own quotes, which arose from deep inside of me and I began to connect to my higher self. I felt I had the enthusiasm and desire to make a difference in the lives of others by sending out positive energy, thoughts and ideas and to communicate with as many hearts and souls as possible.

The positive feedback, encouragement and gratitude from my friends all over the world have been in the hundreds.

In the quotes I have provided to you, there are 'Positive Affirmations' which convert a short message into a personal conviction. An affirmation is a declaration that something is true. What vibrated as a true statement for me at the time of writing these quotes, transpired into a simple affirmation, thus further extracting the essence of what the quote had to convey.

My Reflection

I suggest you read each affirmation after your mind is quiet and calm, and truly reflect on its meaning. Carry the positive message of each quote throughout your day, repeating each affirmation as necessary. Whenever you need a boost of energy, a fresh thought to guide you on the challenges you may be facing, or if you simply need a shift in your consciousness to get in touch with your true self - a spiritual being having a temporary human experience – open my book, relax, take a deep breath and read a quote. With your eyes closed and a smile on your face repeat the positive affirmation out loud. Notice how the heaviness is alleviated from your being.

My wish for you is that you be at peace, find your place of happiness, and that you live a joyous life in a world where everyone lives in a state of higher consciousness in harmony and love.

Feed your soul with healthy thoughts – Namaste,

Rod Pezeshki

Please visit our web pages:

www.livewithpassion.me
www.facebook.com/drshahrad
www.facebook.com/drshahrad#!/DrRod26

My Reflection

The fear (False Expectations Appearing Real) of uncertainty can be debilitating. Notice that fear is only mind and ego created. Be present to every negative thought that is creating it and replace those thoughts with pure FAITH.

<u>Affirmation</u>

"I know the higher purpose of my soul for today"

My Reflection

_____
_____
_____
_____
_____
_____

"You feel good not because the world is right, but your world is right because you feel good!"...Dr. Wayne Dyer

Affirmation

"I open to receive the divine seeds of inspiration that bring optimism, hope and faith. I trust I have everything I need, in every moment."

My Reflection

"Be more concerned with your character than your reputation, because your character is who you really are, while your reputation is merely what others think you are"...John Wooden

Affirmation

"I invite and allow good to come into my life"

My Reflection

Don't underestimate your power to change somebody's world by simple acts of kindness, a bit of caring, a smile, or a silent prayer towards them.......this goes a very long way and really be grateful for being this way ....Do it!

<u>Affirmation</u>

"I have loving and caring thoughts for others".

My Reflection

**Right now, today, just be yourself and be kind
and loving to your inner child**

<u>Affirmation</u>

"I do what I love all the time. My work is my play."

My Reflection

_____

_____

_____

_____

_____

_____

Look back and see what decisions have brought you here.....Look forward & plan where you want to go...However, both require your complete commitment and persistent in the present moment! Enjoy the journey and life NOW!

Affirmation

"I follow my life purpose as it unfolds from moment to moment. I choose my highest path each moment."

My Reflection

**Take a journey within and look at simple ways
you can change yourself for the better. It's truly
the smallest acts that can make a huge
difference in your life and others around you!**

Affirmation

"I am part of a whole, a piece of divine being. I trust
myself."

My Reflection

Cultivate an attitude of positive expectancy about what will happen in the future regardless of what has happened in the past

Affirmation

"I honor my connection to my guide with my words and actions."

My Reflection

Everything we experience as a Problem is in our Mind, the Solution to it is right there also! Change takes place from inside>>>>>OUT not the other way around!

<u>Affirmation</u>

"My mind is open. I love to think in new and higher ways."

_____

My Reflection

Transformation is taking away the veil that covers your true essence who is a loving, caring, beautiful, powerful, confident, worthy, independent, and a happy person. Let your guards down, and let your beauty shine!!!!

<u>Affirmation</u>

"I choose beliefs that bring me aliveness, growth, prosperity, peace, and love in my life. Now is the time!"

My Reflection

When you don't achieve your goal, keep on trying, keep on believing in yourself, and be flexible to change your approach."A quitter never wins-and a winner never quits". Napoleon Hill

Affirmation

"I find my life's work by looking within rather than without."

My Reflection

It's real easy to get caught up in our minds and miss the little simple things that can bring tons of pleasure and happiness......Make a little shift to notice them.

Affirmation

"I'm peaceful and serene. I allow myself to just be!"

My Reflection

"In all human affairs there are efforts, and there are results, and the strength of the effort is the measure of the result."....James Allen

<u>Affirmation</u>

"I stay open to life and accomplish effortlessly"

My Reflection

Listen to the wisdom of your heart. Everyone goes through challenging times in their life. When you feel like you are at the end of the rope, just put the rope down! Believing in yourself and trusting in your source through faith will pull you through the tough times

Affirmation

"I make positive changes in myself purposefully and consciously. I am in charge of my destiny by owning my choices"

My Reflection

Trusting yourself is trusting the source that created you.....once you are at peace, you can be alone, but never feel lonely, and always have the feeling of belonging to something that's much bigger than who you think you are!

Affirmation

"I am infinite and universal and I trust in the divine power of the universe, which is also within me"

My Reflection

Own your mistakes and move on....Responsibility opens the gate to possibility!

<u>Affirmation</u>

"I attract and allow abundance & success into my life because that is who I am"

My Reflection

Silence and the NOW are eternal---Jump right in!

<u>Affirmation</u>

"I love all my emotions. I let my emotions flow
through me."

My Reflection

Smile at life and life will smile right back at you!

Affirmation

"I live in a peaceful universe, in my world nothing ever goes wrong"

My Reflection

Whenever you have any sort of conflict or challenge, think of your source energy at that moment.....see what happens...Let Go and Let God..

<u>Affirmation</u>

"I am safe in the presence of all my challenges"

My Reflection

23

Look at how you can shift your attention when you're interacting with your loved ones; being present makes the experience much sweeter than trapped in your own brain chatter!

<u>Affirmation</u>

"I am calm, alert, and balanced!"

My Reflection

Loving relationships work because there is no work! If you're facing personal challenges, remember that no matter how thin you slice it, there are always two sides to things.

Affirmation

"I live in a state of LOVE"

My Reflection

_____

_____

_____

_____

_____

_____

Open your heart and be ready to receive all the great blessings that manifests for you at all times!

<u>Affirmation</u>

"I intend to have an attitude of gratitude."

My Reflection

"The most wasted of all days is one without laughter."…. E. E. Cummings

<u>Affirmation</u>

"My body is filled with joy and aliveness."

My Reflection

"By letting it go it all gets done. The world is won
by those who let it go. But when you try and try.
The world is beyond
the winning."....Lao Tzu

<u>Affirmation</u>

"I speak of success and prosperity. My words uplift
and inspire others."

My Reflection

Life is a Gift; enjoy opening it as it unfolds moment by moment in front of you

Affirmation

"I find my life's work by looking within rather than without."

My Reflection

**"Always give more than you expect to receive.
The secret of living is giving!"...Anthony Robbins**

<u>Affirmation</u>

"I attract and allow abundance and success into my
life because that's who I am."

My Reflection

Unconditional love comes from within. Carry on a peaceful vision for entire humanity

<u>Affirmation</u>

"I send love to my fears. My fears are the places within me that await my love."

My Reflection

_____

_____

_____

_____

_____

_____

We always have choices....You can give up or choose to live life to its fullest one day at a time, one challenge at a time.

<u>Affirmation</u>

"I know my value. I honor my worth."

My Reflection

Positive thinking is nothing but just the power to believe....As you believe so, the possibilities are endless, as you believe, so it's created.

<u>Affirmation</u>

"I commit to my path. I choose aliveness and growth."

My Reflection

Doing small simple things in any relationship can have profound positive long term effects.......Cherish those seemingly insignificant moments because life's too short!

My Reflection

Your heart has a magnificent magnetic energy field that's fueled by the most powerful force called LOVE; open your heart and let LOVE conquer your world!

<u>Affirmation</u>

"I let love to flow out of me freely."

My Reflection

"Simple kindness to one's self and all that lives is the most powerful transformational force of all "... David Hawkins

<u>Affirmation</u>

"I create what I want easily and effortlessly."

My Reflection

Real friends don't need to do much in order for you to appreciate their presence in your life.

Affirmation

"I always look for ways to make the other person a winner. As I help others win, I win as well"

My Reflection

"Peace cannot be kept by force; it can only be achieved by understanding."....Albert Einstein

<u>Affirmation</u>

"I use every experience as an opportunity to grow."

My Reflection

Having game excellence in anything requires us to raise our standards and change our beliefs into possibilities......Just go for it!

My Reflection

_____

_____

_____

_____

_____

_____

What are you really grateful and happy about? Focus on this simple question when everything feels to be upside down and you're in resistance with what IS...>...NOW...>...LIFE...!

<u>Affirmation</u>

"I trust myself and the universe to flow with synchronicity".

My Reflection

Step up to set yourself up for the highest standards and principles, what you think about becomes your reality.

Affirmation

"I radiate self-esteem, inner peace, love, well-being, and happiness."

My Reflection

_____

_____

_____

_____

_____

_____

"Kindness in giving creates LOVE!"....Lao Tzu

<u>Affirmation</u>

"I allow love to flow in my life. I give and receive Love unconditionally."

My Reflection

Imagine a world with love, joy, peace, and full of compassion where everyone lives in a state of happiness and bliss.....It all starts with you.....Just imagine.

<u>Affirmation</u>

"I am relaxed and at peace with the world and myself."

My Reflection

You are the source of all your emotions. Practicing present moment awareness is a sure way to shift into a positive direction.

<u>Affirmation</u>

"I believe in myself and my path."

My Reflection

Get your emotional fitness suit and put on your positive thinking hat, we're gonna go dance among the stars and conquer the world!

Affirmation

"As I observe my thoughts in the present moment, I only attract positivity and flow effortlessly"

My Reflection

Hey, you don't have to achieve to be happy, you can happily achieve. Go ahead, bliss out, put on a smile, and chill. No one's looking!

<u>Affirmation</u>

"Happiness is my natural state. Not to be happy is failing to connect to your natural being"

My Reflection

I'm learning to control my mind and not allow negative thoughts to penetrate it simply by being an observer rather than judging everything. Real happiness is already here if you get out of your own way and just be!

<u>Affirmation</u>

"If you can go through your day, beginning to end, with loving thoughts, you will become that person who listens to stories of disaster rather than having them."...Louise Hay

My Reflection

A caring friend not only guides you in knowing what to do, but also inspires you to doing what you know!

Affirmation

"I focus on what is good in people, thus assisting them in achieving it."

My Reflection

Take one limiting belief about yourself and turn it around to your advantage today; remember, if you'd have to decide between being Right or being Kind with the people you love, Just pick KIND, it'll stretch a very long way.

Affirmation

"I create what I want with energy. Good things come to me easily."

My Reflection

A wise man asked God, "What's the Meaning of life?" God replied, "Life has no meaning. It is an opportunity given to you to give life a meaning."

<u>Affirmation</u>

"I focus steadily on my vision, higher purpose and goals, knowing that as I do, I create them."

My Reflection

Be committed to yourself, to your health, and to your growth...Live a purposeful life with passion in whatever you put your mind to!

<u>Affirmation</u>

"I choose happiness over despair, laughter over cry, and peace over dis-harmony."

My Reflection

_____

_____

_____

_____

_____

_____

The most incredible feeling is knowing in your heart of hearts that whatever happens is what is suppose to happen; even if we may think it's something "Bad", we must know that the Universal source energy brings to you that which is best for you and your soul to evolve; Trust that it's for your higher good.

<u>Affirmation</u>

"I allow and attract abundance, success, health, joy, love, and peace into my life because that's who I am!"

My Reflection

Being a perceiver rather than judging quickly is a major key to constant happiness...Try it, let things be before you rapidly come to any conclusion.

<u>Affirmation</u>

"Relax....let go....trust.....allow.....enjoy......"

My Reflection

Loving relationships starts by loving yourself first!

Affirmation

"I love myself for all that I am"

My Reflection

When one thing goes wrong, we tend to focus on what's lacking....However, in that moment realize that there's nothing lacking, focus on everything else that's going right for you, have gratitude and move forward!

Affirmation

"I make changes purposefully and consciously. I am in charge of my destiny."

My Reflection

Every moment that you are upset over things that you have no control over is a loss. True joy is one conscious thought away, it's there, just claim it.

My Reflection

Let gratitude nourish every cell in your body. Enjoy being around your loved ones. Have tons of fun with your family and friends. Most important though is to extend a helping hand to those in need.

<u>Affirmation</u>

"I'm grateful for everything that I have and everything that I am."

My Reflection

The essence and beauty of entire existence is you. Stop looking outside for answers. Love and Peace

<u>Affirmation</u>

"I replace all negative thoughts with positive ones."

My Reflection

Why is it more difficult for a person to change and let go of their story than holding on to their own limiting BS (belief system) so tightly? It's incredible! Could it be fear? Learned helplessness? Or, a simple lack of knowledge? Something to think about!

<u>Affirmation</u>

"I trust in myself and let go of my story"

My Reflection

It's not necessary to "Try" so much for proving yourself.....Being aware of your existence brings out infinite calmness and self confidence without trying....Remember that who we ARE communicates far more eloquently than what we Do or Say ...Love and Peace.

Affirmation

"I am at peace with the universe & allow abundance, success, health, and happiness into my life because that's who I AM"

My Reflection

"The best way to pay for a lovely moment is to enjoy it." Richard Bach

<u>Affirmation</u>

"I'm true to my word"

My Reflection

When you view life from a larger Perspective and realize that you are part of a Whole, your problems will Shrink in size, Allowing you to be part of the Solution rather than victim of their Effects.

<u>Affirmation</u>

"Wherever your Focus goes, Energy Flows: I focus on health, happiness, love, joy, peace, and compassion because that's who I AM"

My Reflection

"Life is about moments; don't wait for them, create them"....Anthony Robbins

<u>Affirmation</u>

"I choose to be in control of my own destiny."

My Reflection

"Before you speak, listen. Before you write, think. Before you spend, earn. Before you invest, investigate. Before you criticize, wait. Before you pray, forgive. Before you quit, try. Before you retire, save. Before you die, give."William A. Ward

<u>Affirmation</u>

I surrender, let go, and allow the power of forgiveness, love, compassion and gratitude to take over my past, present, and the future

---

My Reflection

**"Your living is determined not so much by what life
brings to you as by the attitude you bring to life;
not so much by what
happens to you as by the way your mind looks at
what happens."....Kahlil Gibran**

Affirmation

"I honor myself in everything I do"

My Reflection

_____

_____

_____

_____

_____

_____

Success comes to those who have a clear vision of what they want, are persistent, and have an attitude of gratitude while taking each small step in their journey!

<u>Affirmation</u>

"A quitter never wins and a winner never quits"...Napoleon Hill

---

My Reflection

66

Are you in constant preparation for a life of greatness and infinite possibilities or stuck in reaction to limited thinking patterns and fear??? It's your choice and the one you could only make by committing yourself to a higher standard!

Affirmation

"I live my life in a state of gratitude, joy, love, peace, and unlimited possibilities for abundance, creativity, and happiness"

My Reflection

There is no such thing as Failure; there are only Results in life...the question is what do we do with the results we get and how do we turn our challenges into opportunities?

Affirmation

"I choose to see life's challenges as a perceiver rather than a judger"

My Reflection

"The chemist who can extract from his heart's elements compassion, respect, longing , patience, regret, surprise, and forgiveness and compound them into one can create that atom which is called LOVE..."....Kahlil Gibran

<u>Affirmation</u>

"I send peaceful, loving thoughts to other people."

My Reflection

Realize that even if you only have One thing going Right in your life and if you have any portion of your health functioning well, you are LUCKY!.....We have a tendency to focus on what is NOT working, thus shift your Focus on the Positive and remain in Gratitude

<u>Affirmation</u>

"I'm grateful for all that I have and all that I AM"

My Reflection

The feeling of belonging, where you feel that you always matter, is one of the most incredible feelings to constantly experience and also give to someone else through spontaneous acts of KINDNESS>>>>>BE KIND AND ALWAYS BELONG

Affirmation

"I am whole and complete as I was created by being KIND to myself and others. I BELONG"

My Reflection

"The pessimist complains about the wind. The optimist expects it to change. The leader adjusts the sails."……John Maxwell

Affirmation

"I take initiative and act upon my higher good to be balanced and peaceful."

My Reflection

Concentrating on resources you have to create rather than something you want to achieve is far more conducive than focusing on what you don't have or wished you had or even worse, why you don't have but others have!

<u>Affirmation</u>

"In the state of gratitude fear dissolves and success is assured."

My Reflection

True NOBILITY is not being better than anybody else, it's about being better than who YOU use to be.....Be KIND.....Be LOVE!

<u>Affirmation</u>

"I live my life on purpose"

My Reflection

Give yourself a hug and a kiss to acknowledge your inner child as you read this. Later, treat yourself to a delicious double scoop chocolate ice cream or perhaps any flavor of your choice!

<u>Affirmation</u>

"I recognize, love, and connect with my inner child with excitement and joy"

My Reflection

We walk in the field of infinite potentiality, meaning that at any moment the choices we make carries infinite outcome to its result, thus, "Give the Universe something to work with", don't think from a space of lack, limitation, scarcity, and fear; rather recognize that the Universe responds to whatever you imagine; why not then imagine health, wealth, happiness, abundance, prosperity, love, joy, and peace?

Affirmation

"I honor my imagination and appreciate whatever I have with complete sense of gratitude!"

My Reflection

Don't leave the Happenings and the Happiness of Today For Tomorrow! Stick to the NOW

<u>Affirmation</u>

"I'm being aware of my awareness!"

My Reflection

"Life is found in the dance between your greatest fears and deepest desires" Anthony Robbins. Take faith as your lead partner and sometimes switch with courage and determination!

<u>Affirmation</u>

"My willingness to change my thinking is changing my life."

My Reflection

"Don't count the days, make the days count!" Did you make your day count today?

<u>Affirmation</u>

"I follow my heart and just let it BE"

My Reflection

"I have a dream....."Envision, dream, and focus on all the possibilities of abundance, health, happiness, love, joy, peace and compassion!!...have the courage to hold this vision for humanity and allow the universe to express everything that's GOOD through YOU!

Affirmation

"I allow everything GOOD, everything Happy, everything Peaceful, everything Abundant and Creative to express through ME".

My Reflection

We always have a choice to either cherish the moment or get lost in our mental jargon! Choose well. It's your life

<u>Affirmation</u>

"My ability to choose for the better keeps on getting stronger. I trust my intuition!"

My Reflection

_____
_____
_____
_____
_____
_____

"Even after all this time the sun never says to the earth, 'you owe me.' Look what happens with a love like that. It lights the whole sky.".....Hafiz

<u>Affirmation</u>

"I let my LOVE shine outward like the sun and touch as many hearts as possible"

My Reflection

"Whether you'll like it or not, the sun will keep on shining. You feel good not because the world is right, but your world is right because you feel good!"...Dr Wayne Dyer

<u>Affirmation</u>

"I'm a unique expression of love and beauty."

My Reflection

"To be able to look back upon one's life in satisfaction is to live twice."... Kahlil Gibran

<u>Affirmation</u>

"I live a life of significance that really matters!"

My Reflection

Nothing in the universe gets lost or destroyed. What we label death is simply a transformational shift in energy form. It's a return movement to an original source of everything that has ever been and will be. There's something in all of us that's eternal and beyond description. This is love!

Affirmation

"I live my life to the fullest, squeezing the last juice of happiness, joy, and love out of my every moment experience NOW.

My Reflection

I choose to take a stand for peace and the knowing that we live in a friendly universe. By being an active participant from this perspective, we can expand our awareness and help others to free themselves from fear/anxiety/pain!

Affirmation

"I walk with faith in the unknown while trusting my source and create a life of significance from NO-THINGNESS."

My Reflection

"Perhaps they are not stars, but rather openings in heaven where the love of our lost ones pours through and shines down upon us to let us know they are happy."...Shoby

Affirmation

"I'm more than my body; I'm a spiritual being having a temporary human experience"

My Reflection

Whenever there are life's challenges, it helps to use "contrast" at times. This is not to compare yourself to others and judge, but using contrast or thinking out of the box can help to make you FOCUS on solutions, be GRATEFUL for WHAT IS, and enable you to keep what you envision TO BE manifest into reality!

Affirmation

"I'm always GOOD ENOUGH"

My Reflection

"Only those who have learned the power of sincere and selfless contribution experience life's deepest joy!"...Anthony Robbins

Affirmation

"I radiate peace and serenity no matter what is going on around me"

My Reflection

Don't underestimate your power to change somebody's world by simple acts of kindness, a bit of caring, a smile, or a silent prayer towards them.......this goes a very long way and really be grateful for being this way ....Do it!

<u>Affirmation</u>

"I have loving and caring thoughts for others".

My Reflection

_____

_____

_____

_____

_____

_____

Life is too short. Make every experience valuable and really enjoy every gift you've been given! True happiness is found in the simplest things.......Peace

<u>Affirmation</u>

"I enjoy and value every second of my existence".

My Reflection

Practice infinite patience, compassion, and understanding towards those that you hold dearest to you; who are the same people that can hurt your feelings the most!

<u>Affirmation</u>

"I forgive, and let go. My priority in life is to be happy"

My Reflection

Nothing is more powerful than connecting at the deepest level with someone you care for, feeling their feelings, and embracing their presence in your life because they are the one who is your true teacher about yourself! Don't judge, stay open and be patient!

Affirmation

"I have infinite patient and love to give. The more I give, the more I receive".

My Reflection

Each one of us has infinite capacity to create goodness and a life that serves for humanities higher purpose. Hold the unique IDEA that you have, one that is wanting to express through you, nurture it, trust it, trust yourself, and let the Universe do it's magic.....Our job is to keep that IDEA sacred, give it love, and always be in gratitude!

Affirmation

"I am awake and aware! I have a clear vision of what wants to manifest through me and trust my purpose in life!"

My Reflection

_____

_____

_____

_____

_____

_____

If you have mixed emotions and looking for answers, look within yourself because the answers you're seeking are already there. No amount of you feeling bad or hurt will change any circumstance other than creating resistance to that which you cherish most>>>>Your own Happiness!

<u>Affirmation</u>

"I respect my emotions, not judging them and allowing space for their expression"

My Reflection

"Sometimes, it's not a bad idea to practice SILENCE and not get into reaction with a loved one who is hurting for whatever reason and venting out on you!.....It's really difficult and I wish I had the skills to remain Silent when it's a Must......hopefully I get there in this life time!"

Affirmation

I forgive and let go...I practice Silence in order to dissolve my EGO

My Reflection

If you think by taking a short cut or the easy way out that you're going to reach your dreams, be what you really deserve to be and achieve success. It's not going to happen!!! You MUST take that extra step, be persistent, be committed, and break through your FEARS!

<u>Affirmation</u>

"I commit myself to highest standards and values, allow that which is already here for my higher good to manifest in my life"

My Reflection

Today, now, start to practice forgiveness because only by forgiving our past and letting go we can create the space of infinite potential and possibility for change, creativity and ever lasting peace!

<u>Affirmation</u>

"I forgive myself and others for any intentional or un-intentional hurtful and painful experiences"

My Reflection

Special Mental Diet: terminate I'm not good enough thoughts, eliminate angry thoughts, disregard pessimistic attitudes, avoid procrastination: HOWEVER, encourage POSITIVE THOUGHTS, adopt I AM ALL That IS. I AM GOOD ENOUGH. Nurture Optimism, welcome LOVE, Passion, Purpose, Abundance, and PEACE as your daily habits!

Affirmation

"I take this mental diet to heart and practice it every day of this year"

My Reflection

_____

_____

_____

_____

_____

_____

Think about what you've been putting off for "later"...make an effort to take one step in action towards doing what you have that intuitive inclination for...whatever it is, give it your focus and energy and let it be...I leave you with this thought!

<u>Affirmation</u>

"I commit to keep my body, mind, and spirit in balance, peace, and harmony at all times!"

My Reflection

Having problems with the voice in your head? No need to visit a psychiatrist because you're not crazy! Just observe the voice. Don't judge it. Have compassion towards it's nonsense and let your stillness create a gap between you the "observer" and you the "automatic chatter"! Stay in BEING.

<u>Affirmation</u>

I'm peaceful and serene, I allow myself to just BE"

My Reflection

I think the biggest responsibility you could take is to forgive yourself and others for something you said that came about from being hurt and from your ego.....at the moment that you are not aware and coming from pain You may say hurtful things to your loved ones and then regret it...Words are Powerful...I'm reminding myself to be mindful of them.

<u>Affirmation</u>

"I'm in a continual completeness. I'm expanding my awareness of it"

My Reflection

Your world around you is nothing more or nothing less than the reflection of what you have become from within-you must become the very things you choose to experience in your life: peace, healing, joy, compassion, and love!

<u>Affirmation</u>

"I live a purposeful life with infinite passion"

My Reflection

Think of this concept: "Gravity is Constant, so is Negativity". Be aware! You must constantly feed your mind positive, nutritious thoughts, meditate, and envision what you want to create that benefit everybody. Taking it easy and letting it slip by even temporarily will cost you what you have worked so hard to achieve; it only takes a small amount of poison to kill someone! So, WATCH your MIND!

<u>Affirmation</u>

"Once I make a decision, all the forces in the universe are mobilized to bring about my highest good."

My Reflection

Be aware of your thoughts the second you are in contact with a stranger, see if you start thinking strange stories, comments, or labeling the other person this or that, good or bad, thin or fat, pretty or ugly, bald or hairy, poor or rich, mean or kind. Point is, be KIND, Don't JUDGE, because you are exactly part of that which you are Judging

<u>Affirmation</u>

I open my heart with compassion and love; let go of my need to be right and let go of needing approval by others.

My Reflection

Listen to the "giving up voice" that finds its way in the corner of your mind. Just be aware and realize that you are stronger, more capable, worthy, more creative, lovely, more gracious, smart, and more determined over any challenges in your life! Be persistent, Be Calm, and have Faith

<u>Affirmation</u>

"I'm bigger than any challenges in my life because I have the universe to back me up"

My Reflection

The only way you can be at peace is to stop fighting with What IS, be Grateful for what Is, Envision a Higher path that you Want to create and take measurable Actions to lead you achieving it. Meanwhile, practice unconditional love towards yourself & others!

<u>Affirmation</u>

"My heart center is radiant with love. I lift others through my love."

My Reflection

Never fight your emotions when they are trying to express themselves...emotions come from the heart, some are painful and some are happy, but each are special gifts trying to guide you in a direction where you should be...shine the painful ones with love and cherish the happy ones with an open heart

Affirmation

"I allow any emotions express through me, without judging myself, rather be grateful to them"

My Reflection

"Success is doing ordinary things extraordinarily well."....Jim Rohn

<u>Affirmation</u>

"I am destined for a successful life"

My Reflection

"Life rewards those who contribute on a massive scale through generosity and giving.......that's what the art of fulfillment is all about!"......Anthony Robbins

<u>Affirmation</u>

"I draw to myself many wonderful opportunities to make a difference in the world.

My Reflection

Rod's Doctrine

1- I am committed to myself, to my health, and to my growth.

2- I am responsible for everything that I do, say, and think.

3- I am confident by making decisions and taking the necessary actions.

4- I am peaceful and serene. I allow myself to just be.

5- I am powerful beyond measures.

6- I am open to new discoveries.

7- I am compassionate and caring towards myself and others.

8- I am courageous and resourceful in every stage of my life.

9- I am persistent and have the desire to accomplish my goals.

10- I am strong. My strength comes from my wisdom and knowledge.

11- I am faithful. My faith comes from my connection to the universal life source energy.

12- I am love. I give and receive love unconditionally.

13- I am grateful for everything that I have and everything that I AM.

My Reflection

My Reflection

16123723R00069

Made in the USA
Middletown, DE
05 December 2014